Read
Trace
Write
a
एक
I
मी
am
आहे
an
एक
as
म्हणून
at
येथे

Read and write the sentence!

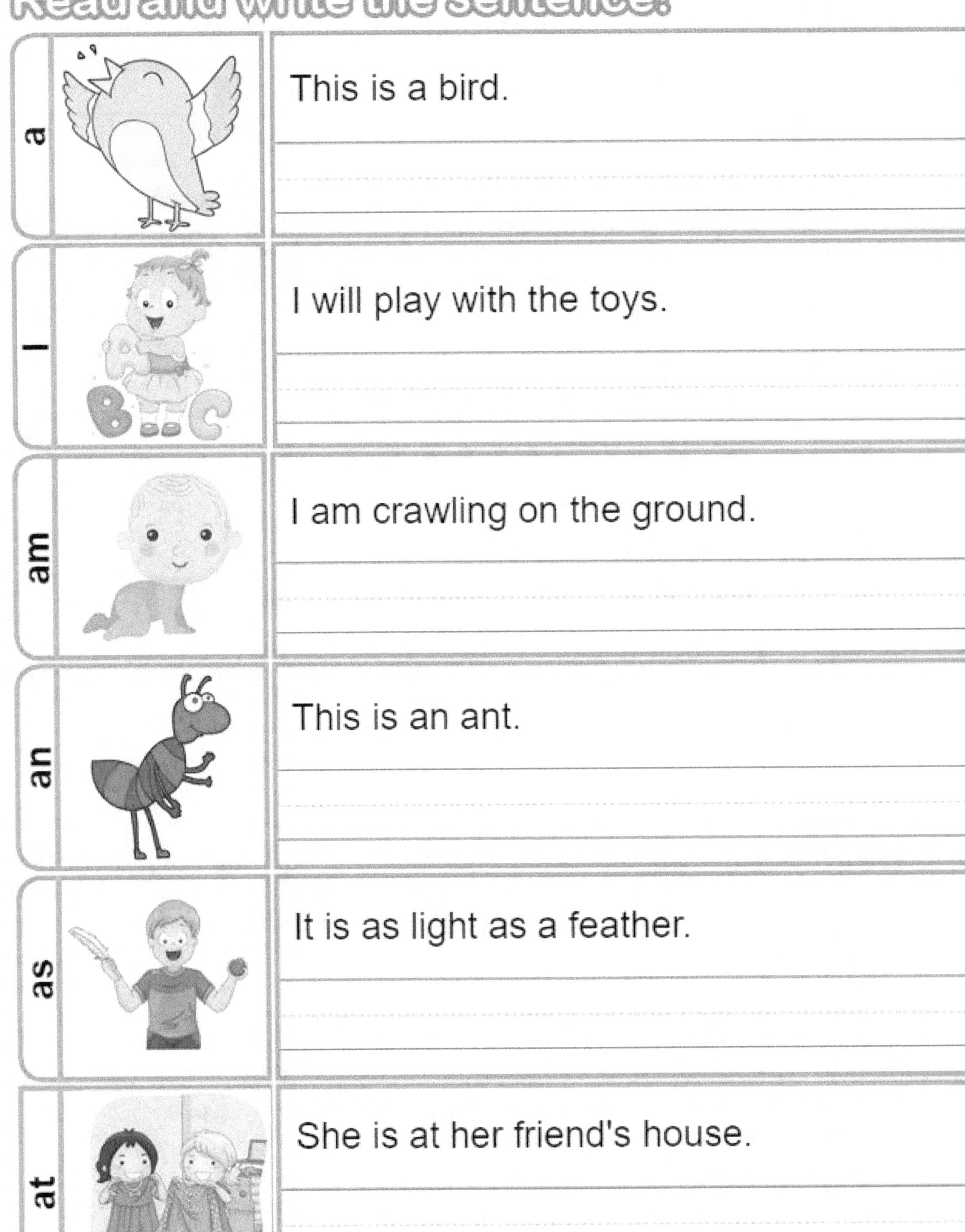

a		This is a bird.
I		I will play with the toys.
am		I am crawling on the ground.
an		This is an ant.
as		It is as light as a feather.
at		She is at her friend's house.

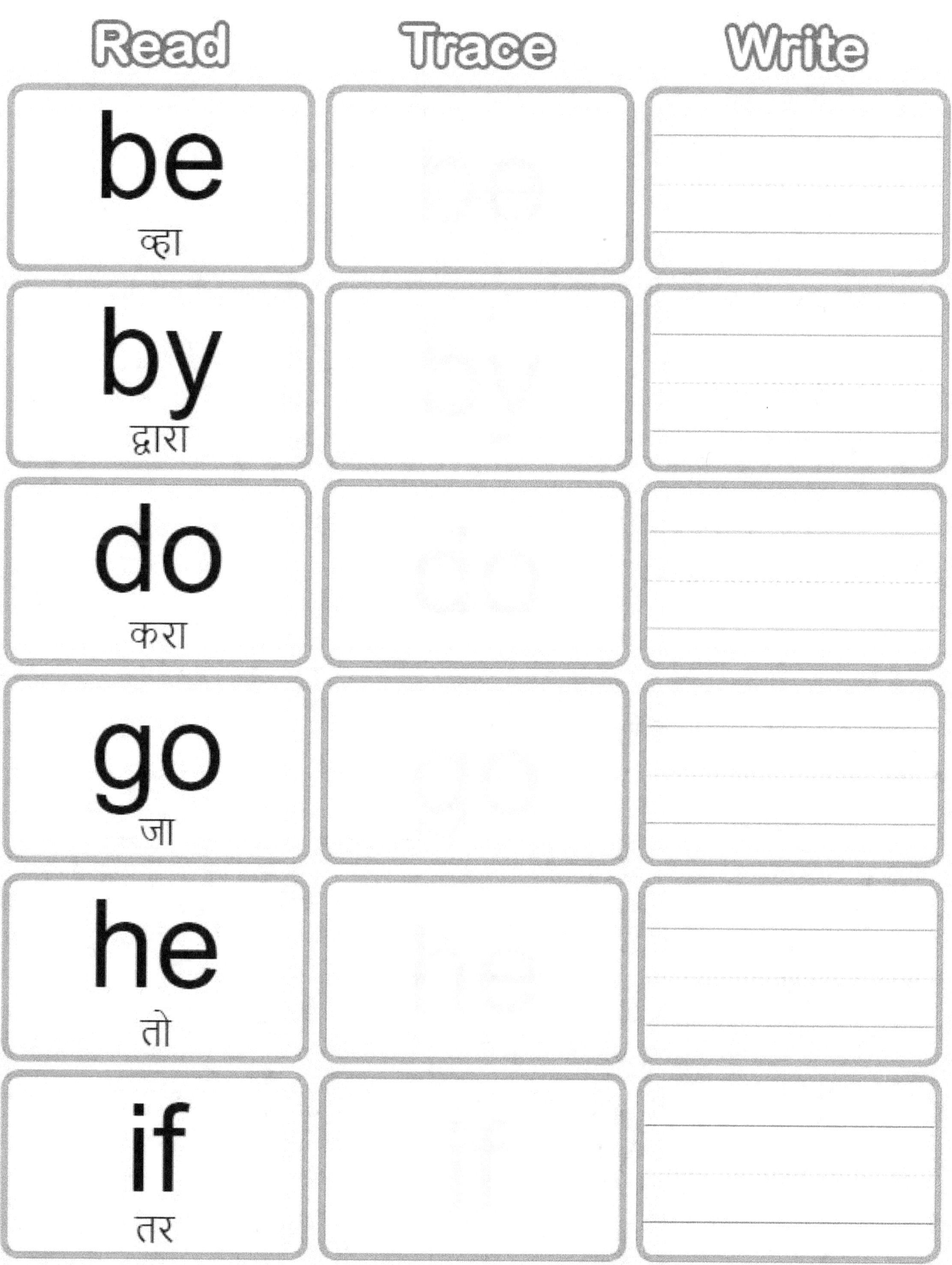

Read
Trace
Write
be
व्हा
by
द्वारा
do
करा
go
जा
he
तो
if
तर

Read and write the sentence!

be	We will be friends.
by	This story is by me.
do	She will do the cleaning.
go	He will go somewhere.
he	He is bored.
if	If I put my clothes here, it will get washed.

Read
Trace
Write
in
मध्ये
is
आहे
it
तो
me
मी
my
माझे
no
नाही

Read and write the sentence!

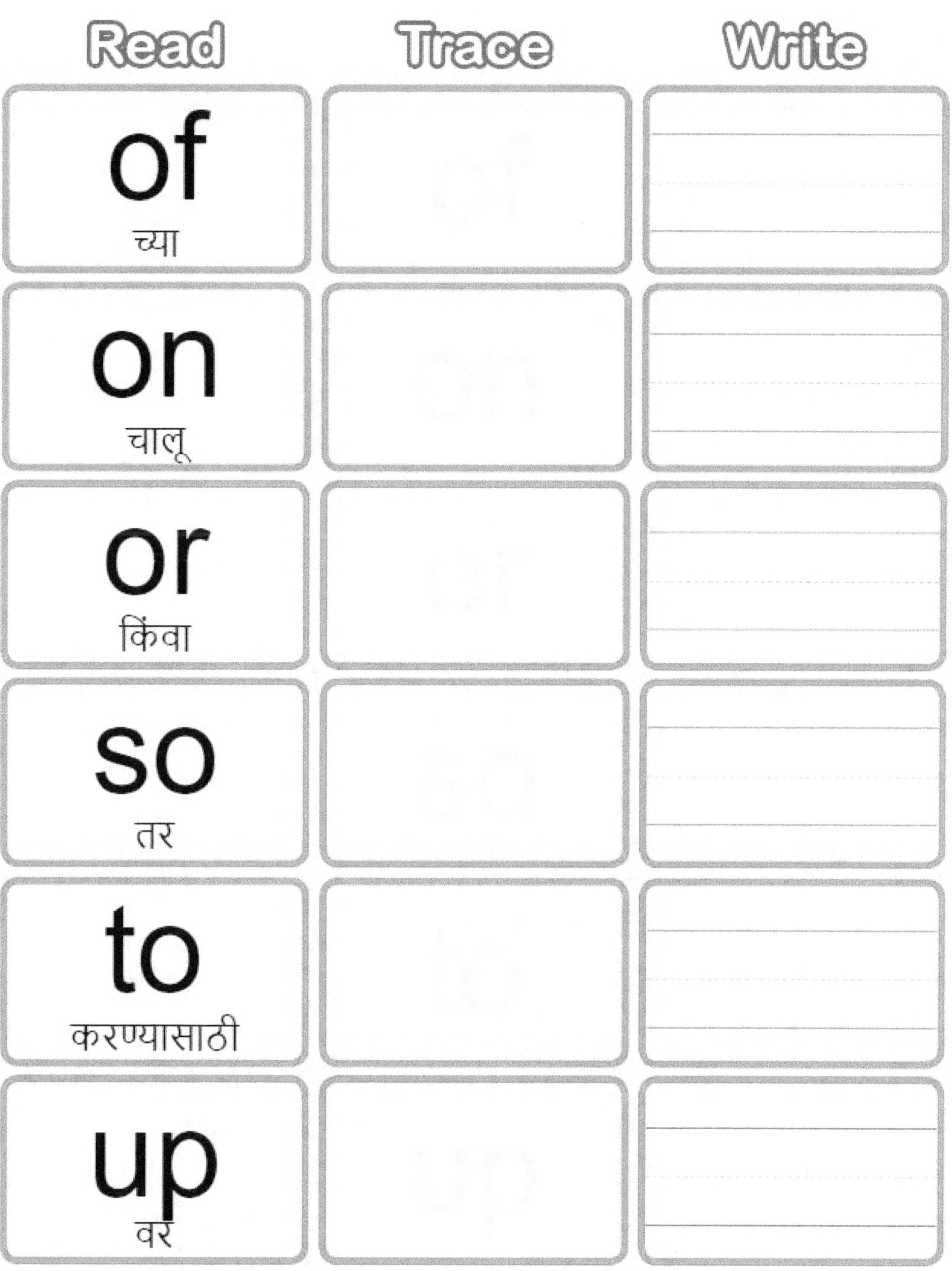

Read
Trace
Write
of
च्या
on
चालू
or
किंवा
so
तर
to
करण्यासाठी
up
वर

Read and write the sentence!

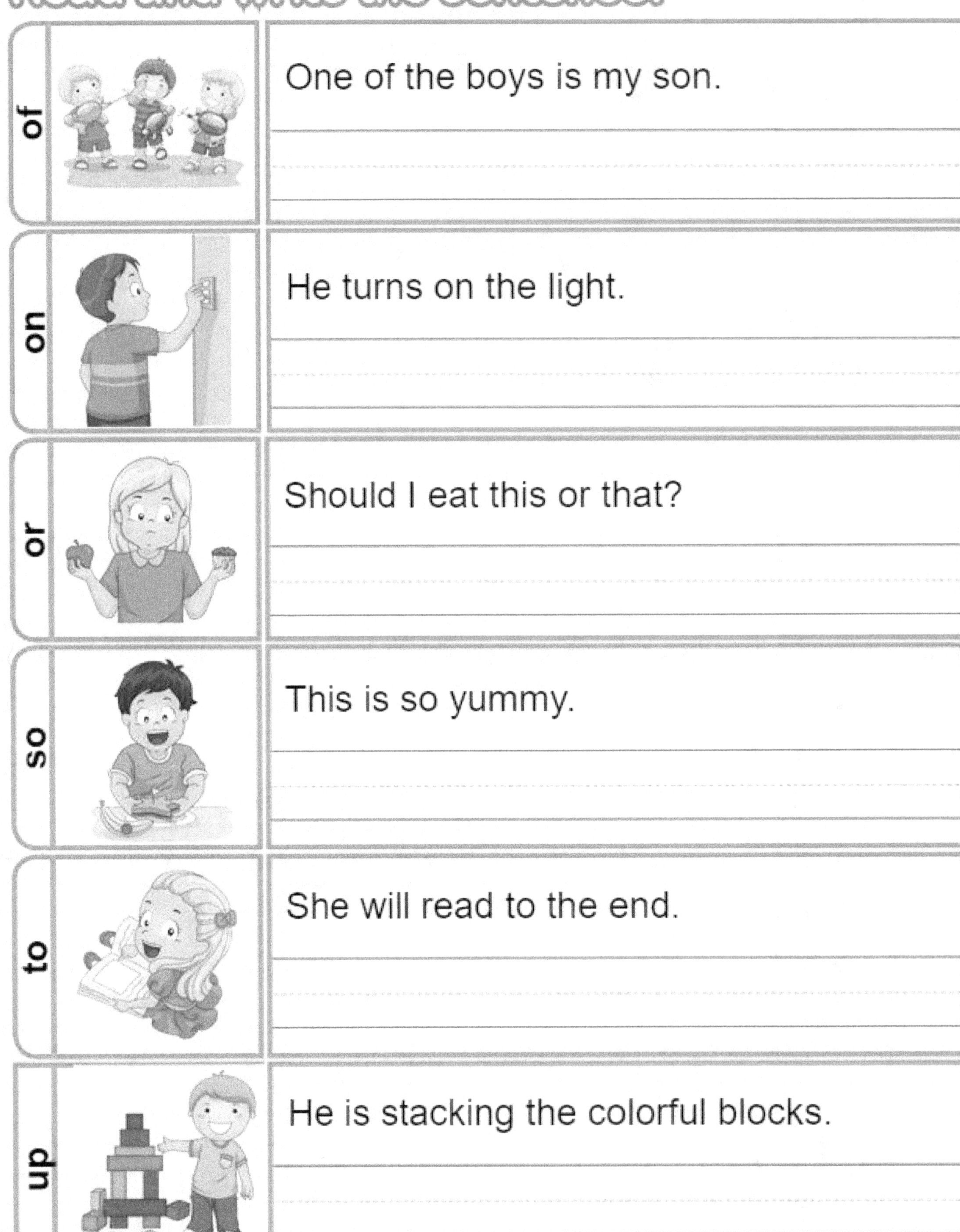

Read	Trace	Write
us आम्हाला		
we आम्ही		
all सर्व		
and आणि		
any कोणत्याही		
are आहेत		

Read and write the sentence!

us		Both of us are walking.
we		We are helping to make a house.
all		We are all dancing together.
and		My brother and I are playing.
any		They can read any books.
are		The eggs are colorful.

Read	Trace	Write
ask विचारा		
ate खाल्ले		
bed बेड		
big मोठा		
box बॉक्स		
boy मुलगा		

Read and write the sentence!

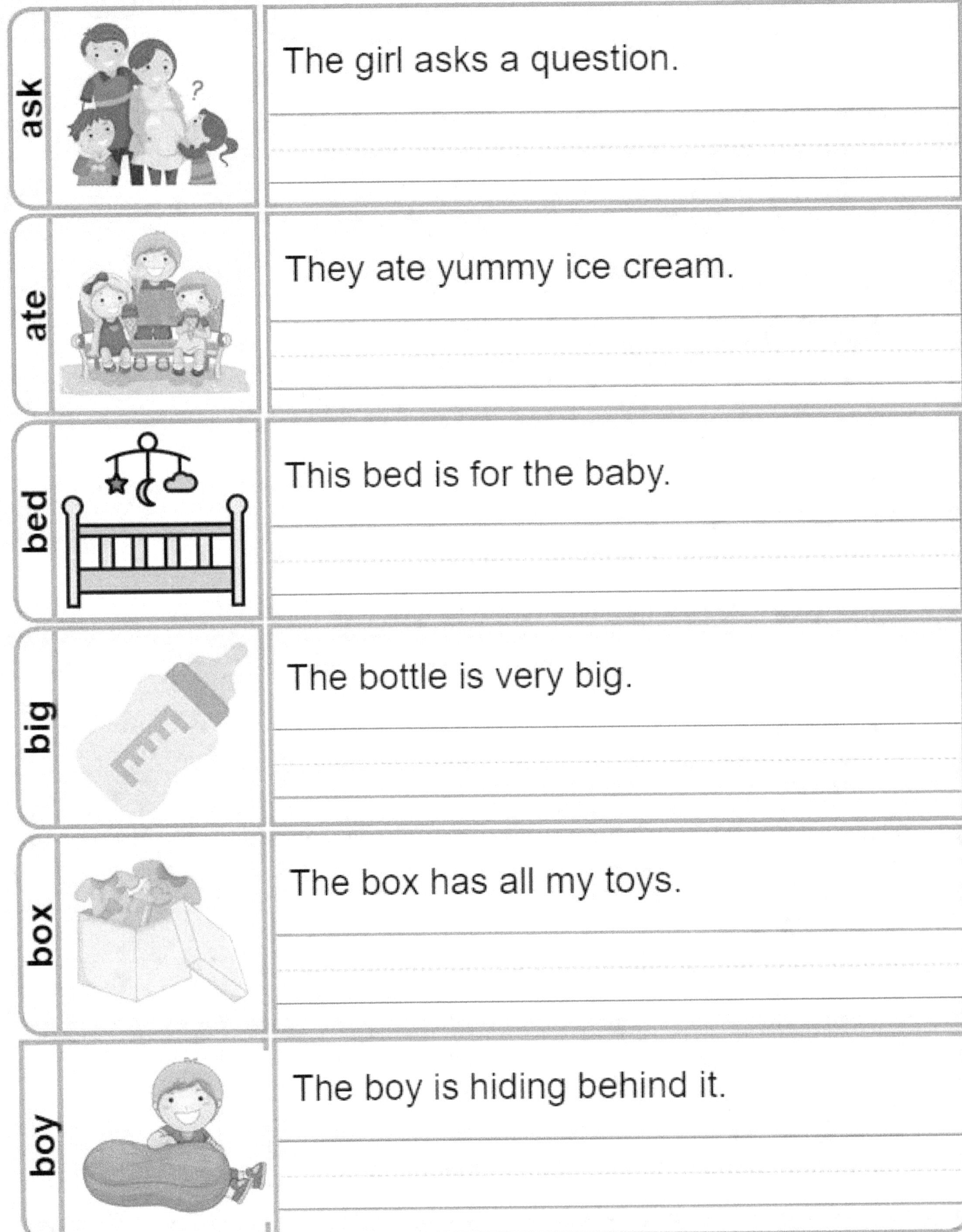

	Sentence
ask	The girl asks a question.
ate	They ate yummy ice cream.
bed	This bed is for the baby.
big	The bottle is very big.
box	The box has all my toys.
boy	The boy is hiding behind it.

Read	Trace	Write
but परंतु		
buy खरेदी		
can करू शकता		
car गाडी		
cat मांजर		
cow गाय		

Read and write the sentence!

but	I want to go, but my son doesn't.
buy	He buys lots of stuff.
can	The baby will drink milk from the can.
car	The car is red.
cat	The cat is sad.
cow	The cow is funny.

Read	Trace	Write
cut कट		
day दिवस		
did केले		
dog कुत्रा		
eat खा		
egg अंडी		

Read and write the sentence!

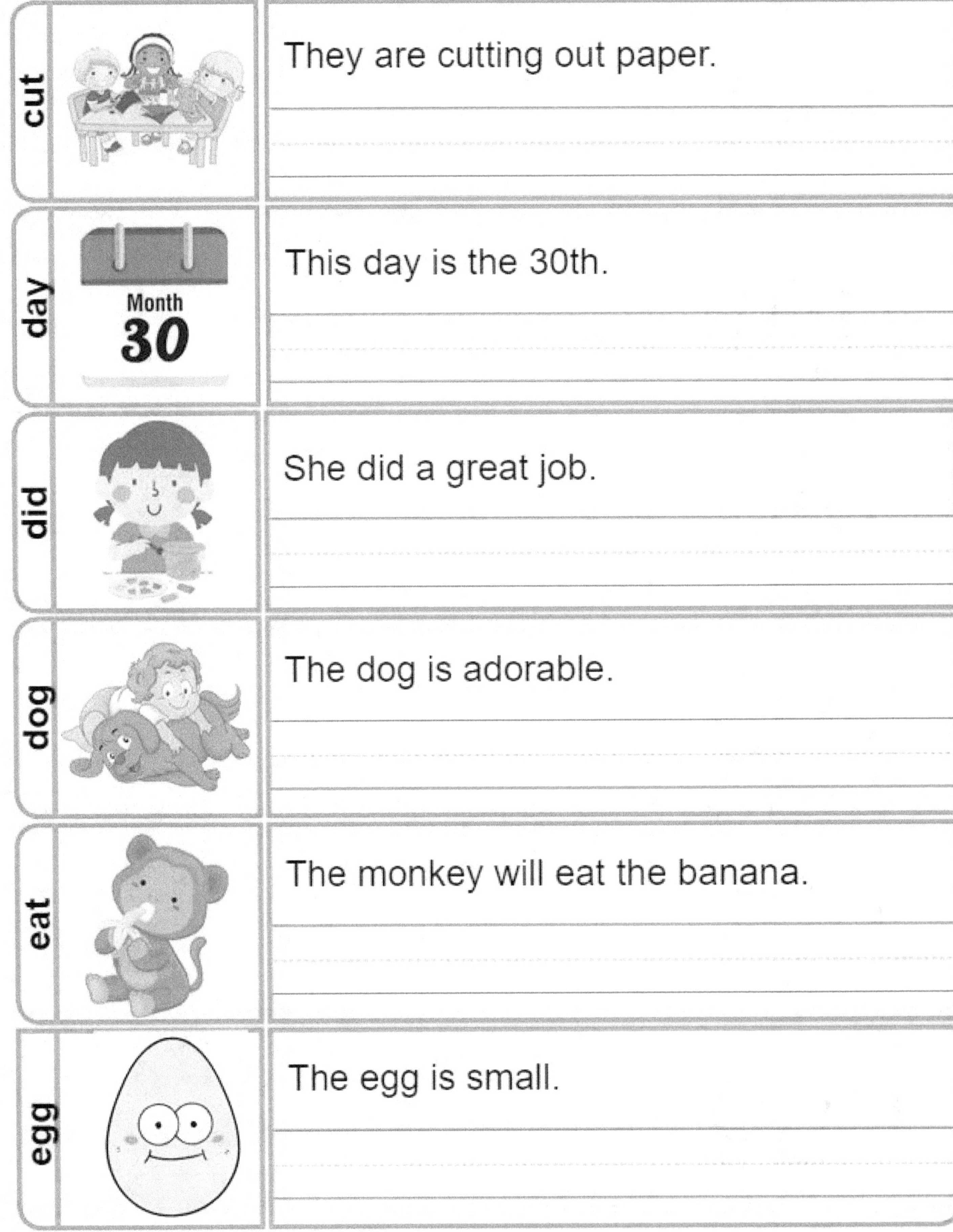

Read
Trace
Write
eye
डोळा
far
आतापर्यंत
fly
उडणे
for
च्या साठी
get
मिळवा
got
आला

Read and write the sentence!

eye		The fox is closing his eyes.
far		He can fly the plane very far.
fly		The bee will fly back home.
for		The dog is begging for food.
get		He will get a trophy.
got		The baby got some new toys.

Read
Trace
Write
had
होते
has
आहे
her
तिला
him
त्याला
his
त्याचा
hot
गरम

Read and write the sentence!

Read
Trace
Write
how
कसे
its
त्याचा
leg
पाय
let
द्या
man
मनुष्य
may
मे

Read and write the sentence!

Read	Trace	Write
men पुरुष		
new नवीन		
not नाही		
now आता		
off बंद		
old जुन्या		

Read and write the sentence!

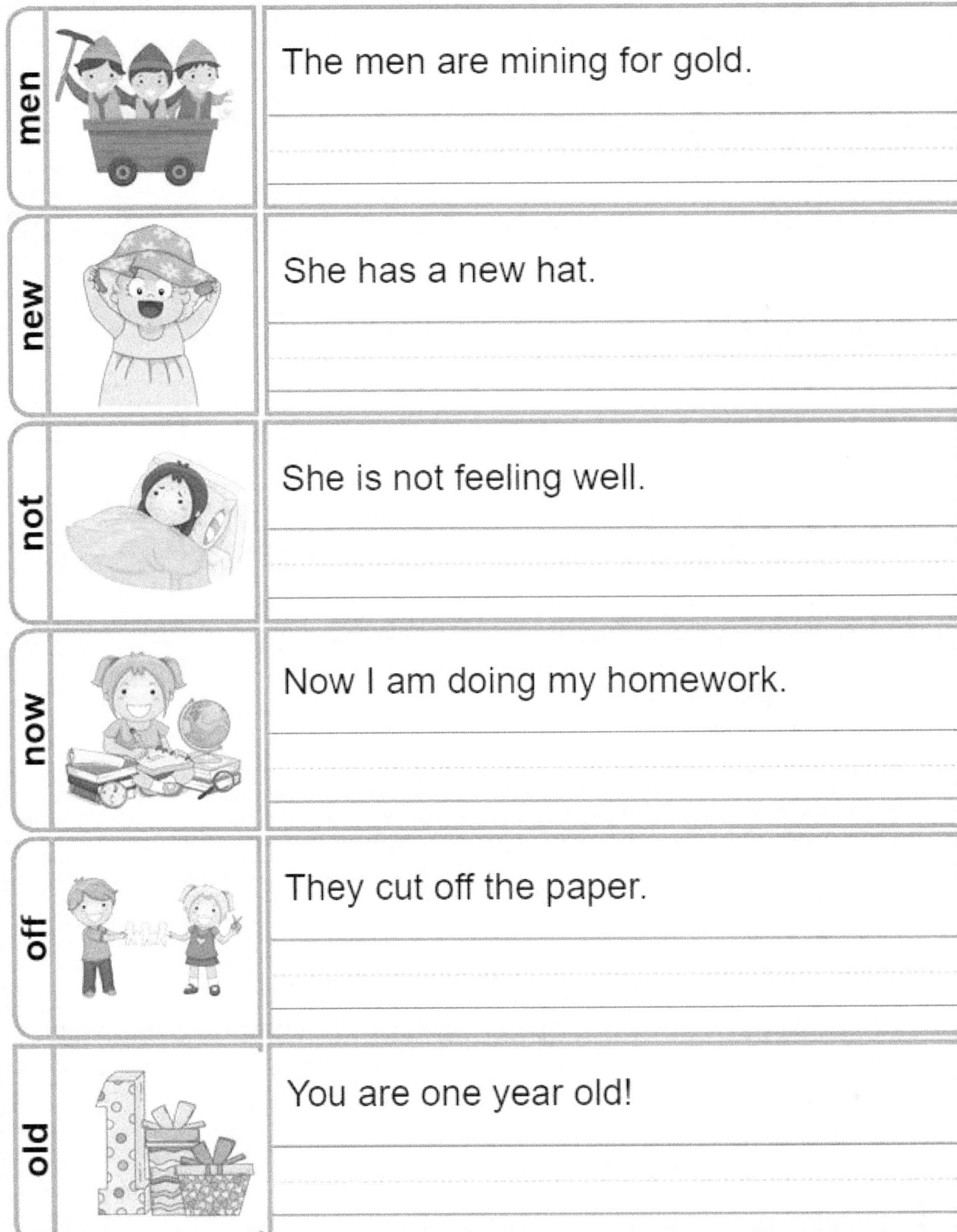

men		The men are mining for gold.
new		She has a new hat.
not		She is not feeling well.
now		Now I am doing my homework.
off		They cut off the paper.
old		You are one year old!

Read
Trace
Write
one
एक
our
आमचे
out
बाहेर
own
स्वत: चे
pig
डुक्कर
put
ठेवले

Read and write the sentence!

one		The panda says one.
our		This is our room.
out		He will go out.
own		The man owns a computer.
pig		She is sleeping on her pig.
put		She is putting an arm around her daughter.

Read	Trace	Write
ran चालवा		
red लाल		
run चालवा		
saw पहा		
say म्हणा		
see पहा		

Read and write the sentence!

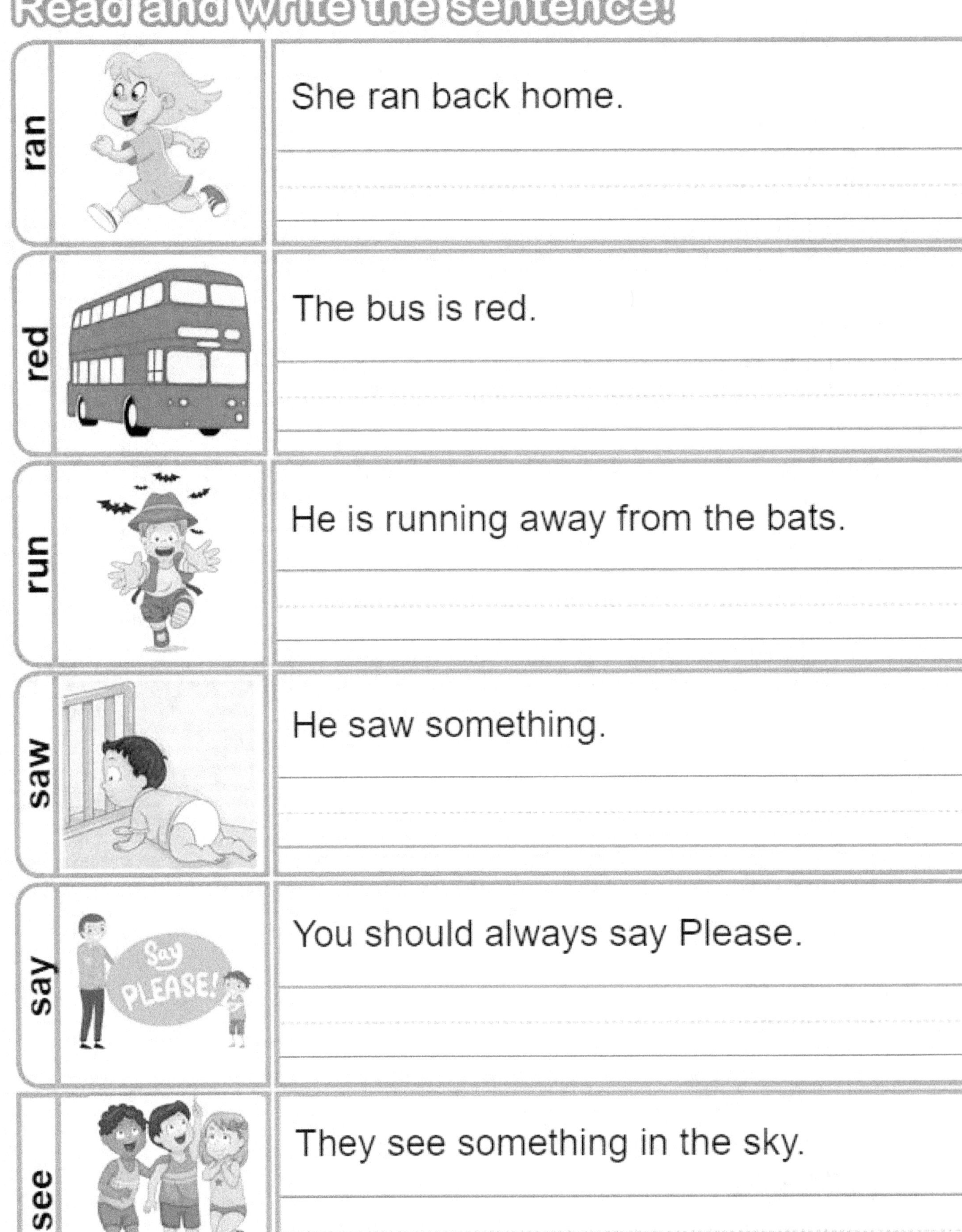

	Sentence
ran	She ran back home.
red	The bus is red.
run	He is running away from the bats.
saw	He saw something.
say	You should always say Please.
see	They see something in the sky.

Read
Trace
Write
she
ती
sit
बसा
six
सहा
sun
सूर्य
ten
दहा
the
एक

Read and write the sentence!

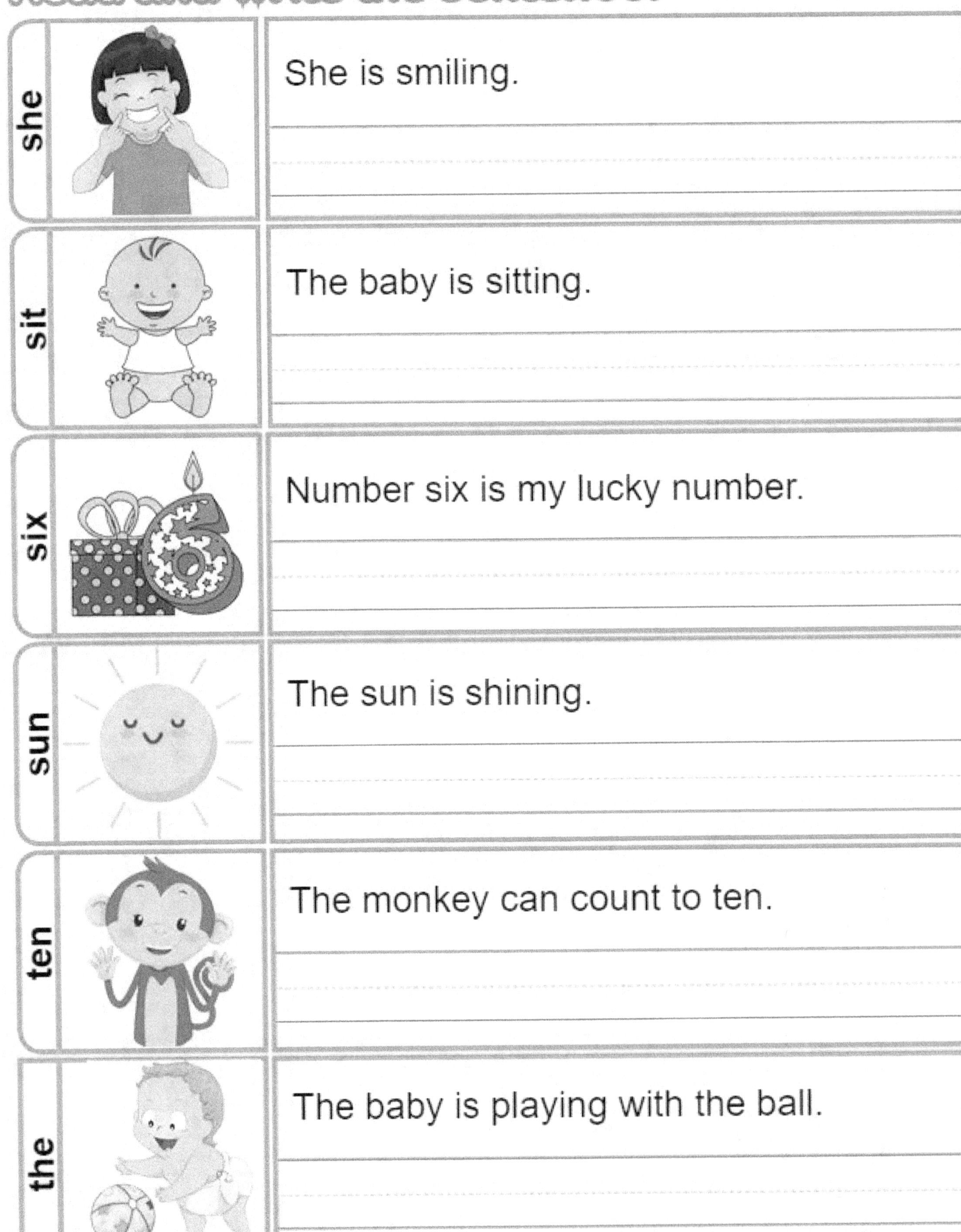

she		She is smiling.
sit		The baby is sitting.
six		Number six is my lucky number.
sun		The sun is shining.
ten		The monkey can count to ten.
the		The baby is playing with the ball.

Read	Trace	Write
too खूप		
top वर		
toy खेळण्याचे		
try प्रयत्न		
two दोन		
use वापरा		

Read and write the sentence!

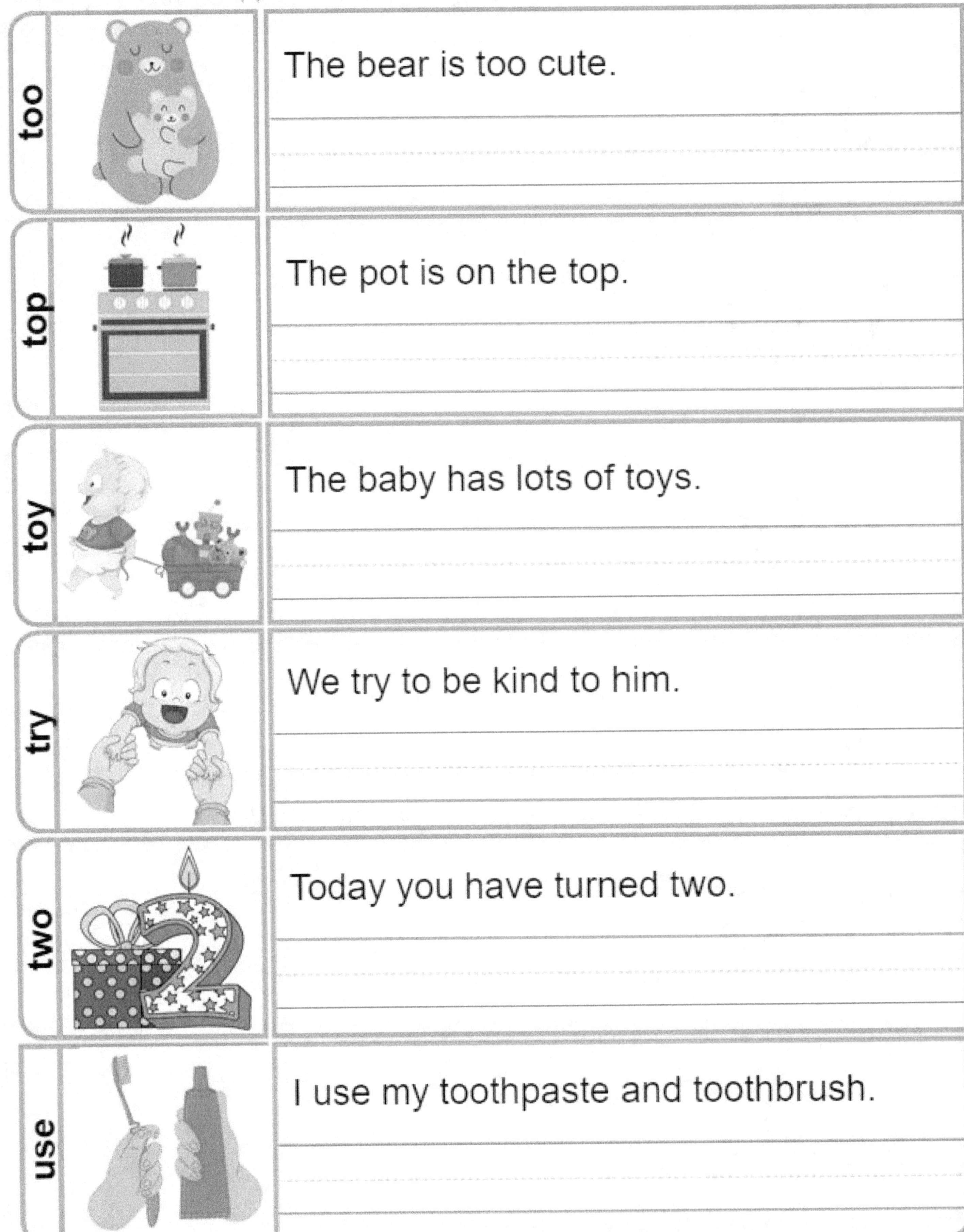

Read
Trace
Write
was
होते
way
मार्ग
who
काय
why
का
yes
होय
you
आपण

Read and write the sentence!

Read	Trace	Write

Read and write the sentence!

away	She is running away.
baby	The baby is playing with her toys.
back	The baby turns her back.
ball	The balls are all over the place.
bear	The bear is holding a present.
been	The baby has been crying.

Read	Trace	Write
bell घंटा		
best सर्वोत्तम		
bird पक्षी		
blue निळा		
boat बोट		
both दोन्ही		

Read and write the sentence!

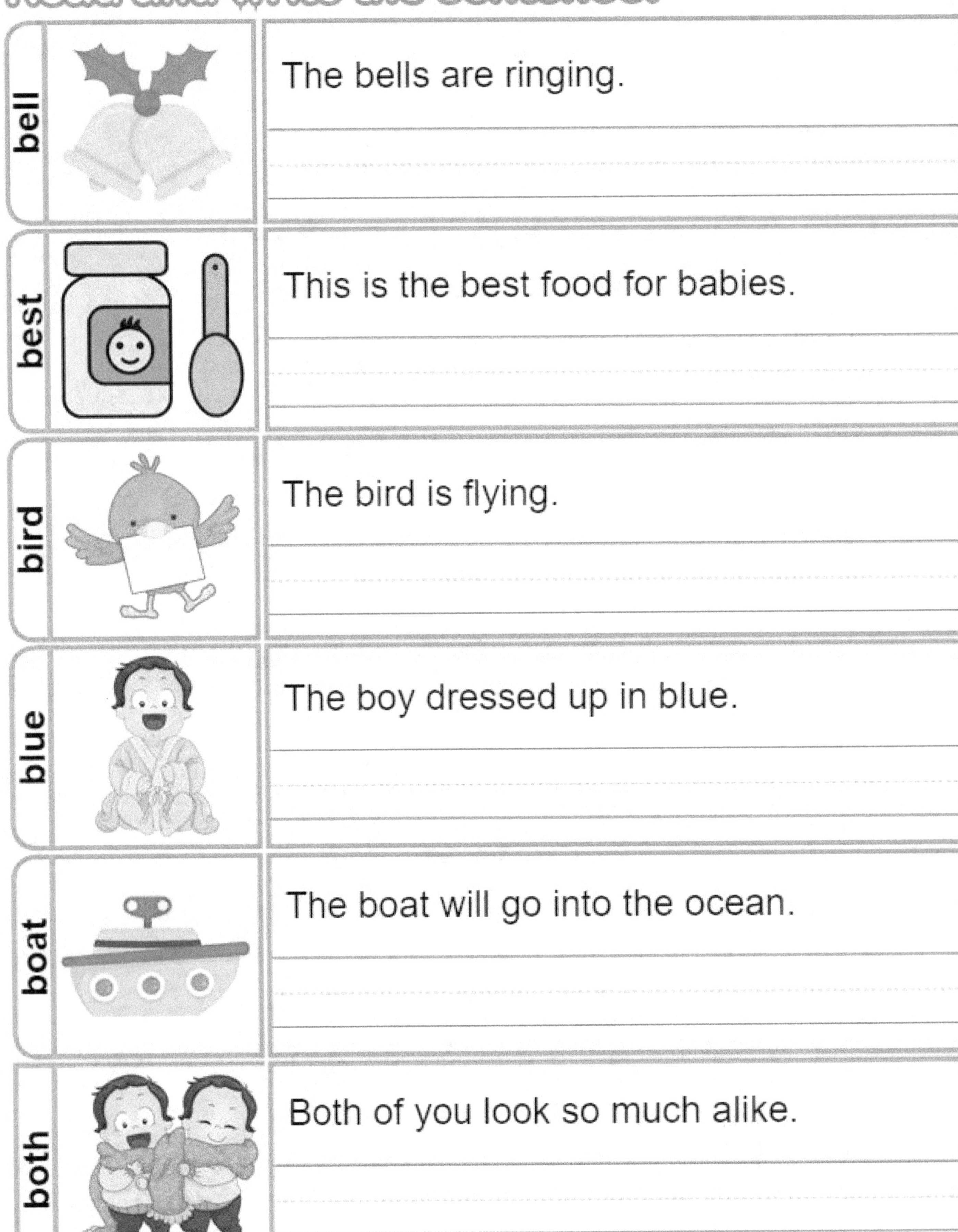

Read	Trace	Write
cake केक		
call कॉल करा		
came आले		
coat कोट		
cold थंड		
come या		

Read and write the sentence!

cake		The cake is for your birthday.
call		She is calling for somebody.
came		She came with her bag.
coat		The girl is wearing her coat.
cold		The baby feels cold.
come		Come here to the slide!

Read
Trace
Write

corn
कॉर्न

does
करते

doll
बाहुली

done
केले

door
दार

down
खाली

Read and write the sentence!

corn	The corn tastes good.
does	Does that thing taste bad?
doll	She is hugging her doll.
done	I've done reading my book.
door	They open the door.
down	The boy turns his head down.

Read	Trace	Write
draw काढा		
duck बदक		
fall पडणे		
farm शेत		
fast वेगवान		
feet पाऊल		

Read and write the sentence!

draw
They all draw pictures.

duck
The duck is yellow.

fall
He fell down from the swing.

farm
He grows crops at his farm.

fast
She is doing everything very fast.

feet
I touch my feet.

Read	Trace	Write

Read and write the sentence!

find	They are finding something.
fire	The fire is blazing and dangerous.
fish	The fish are swimming in the ocean.
five	You get birthday gifts for turning five.
four	The lion is turning four today.
from	She will draw a picture of her flower.

Read
Trace
Write
full
पूर्ण
game
खेळ
gave
दिली
girl
मुलगी
give
द्या
goes
जाते

Read and write the sentence!

full	His backpack is full of things.
game	This game is enjoyable.
gave	She gave something to her friend.
girl	The girl is sad because of something.
give	The baby gives her mommy something.
goes	She goes to the forest.

Read
Trace
Write
here
येथे
hill
टेकडी
hold
धरा
home
मुख्यपृष्ठ
hurt
दुखापत
into
मध्ये

Read and write the sentence!

here	America is over here.
hill	The hill has some trees and a house.
hold	He is holding his daughter.
home	He drew a picture of his home.
hurt	The boy is hurt.
into	He will jump into the pool.

Read
Trace
Write
jump
उडी
just
फक्त
keep
ठेवा
kind
दयाळू
know
माहित आहे
like
आवडले

Read and write the sentence!

jump		The cat jumped on the cushion.
just		The arrival of the plane just arrived.
keep		She keeps thinking about it.
kind		The woman is kind to the girl.
know		They know that they will go over there.
like		He likes to ride on the horse.

Read	Trace	Write
live राहतात		
long लांब		
look दिसत		
made केले		
make केले		
many अनेक		

live	They all live together.
long	The pencil is very long.
look	They are looking at something.
made	They made a promise.
make	They are going to make something.
many	He has many shirts.

Read   Trace   Write

Read	Trace	Write
milk दूध		
much जास्त		
must हे केलेच पाहिजे		
name नाव		
nest घरटे		
once एकदा		

Read and write the sentence!

milk		I have milk for breakfast.
much		I like to eat this very much.
must		I must do all my homework.
name		My name is Joe.
nest		The bird has a nest.
once		He once liked to look at his computer.

Read	Trace	Write
only फक्त		
open उघडा		
over प्रती		
pick निवडा		
play खेळा		
pull खेचा		

Read and write the sentence!

only	There is only one student.
open	He wants to open the door.
over	The class is over.
pick	She picked up something.
play	They like to play together.
pull	She is pulling on her friend's hair.

<table>
<tr><th>Read</th><th>Trace</th><th>Write</th></tr>
<tr><td>rain
पाऊस</td><td></td><td></td></tr>
<tr><td>read
वाचा</td><td></td><td></td></tr>
<tr><td>ride
चालविणे</td><td></td><td></td></tr>
<tr><td>ring
रिंग</td><td></td><td></td></tr>
<tr><td>said
म्हणाले</td><td></td><td></td></tr>
<tr><td>seed
बियाणे</td><td></td><td></td></tr>
</table>

Read and write the sentence!

rain	The rain is not going to hit us.
read	She likes to read books.
ride	The baby is riding on a toy horse.
ring	The bird is holding a ring in its beak.
said	She said hello to her neighbor.
seed	The seeds are going to plant.

Read
Trace
Write
shoe
बूट
show
दाखवा
sing
गाणे
snow
बर्फ
some
काही
song
गाणे

Read and write the sentence!

shoe	Her shoes are cute and purple.
show	This map shows the location.
sing	The baby can sing along.
snow	I like to play snow.
some	These are some of my toys.
song	I will sing a song in the talent show.

Read	Trace	Write
soon लवकरच		
stop थांबा		
take घ्या		
tell सांगा		
that ते		
them त्यांना		

Read and write the sentence!

soon		The eggs will hatch soon.
stop		The teacher says to stop.
take		They take some flowers.
tell		She is telling a story.
that		That bird dressed up as Santa.
them		He likes to eat them.

Read
Trace
Write

then
मग
they
ते
this
हे
time
वेळ
tree
झाड
upon
यावर

Read and write the sentence!

then		Then, I will go to bed.
they		They are running to school.
this		This is my duck.
time		The time always moves on.
tree		There are lots of green trees in the park.
upon		Once upon a time, there was a princess.

Read	Trace	Write
very खूप		
walk चाला		
want पाहिजे		
warm उबदार		
wash धुवा		
well चांगले		

Read and write the sentence!

very		The baby is lovely.
walk		They are walking on the sidewalk.
want		The baby wants more milk.
warm		The bath is warm.
wash		She is going to wash the dishes.
well		He can save money well.

Read
Trace
Write
went
गेला
were
आहेत
what
काय
when
कधी
will
होईल
wind
वारा

Read and write the sentence!

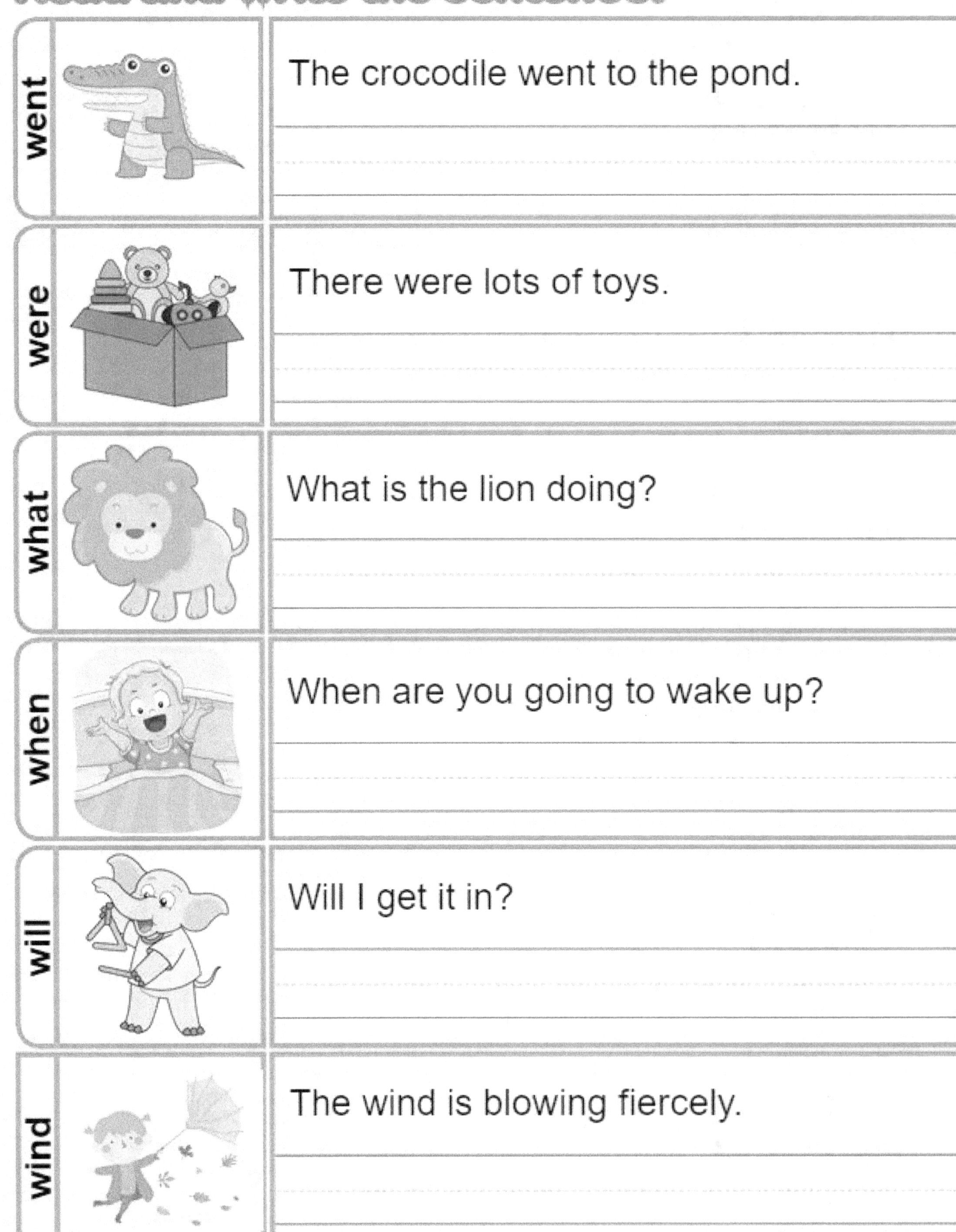

Read	Trace	Write
wish इच्छा		
with सह		
wood लाकूड		
work काम		
your आपले		
about बदल		

Read and write the sentence!

wish	I wish you a happy Christmas!
with	He is with his sister.
wood	He is stacking up wooden blocks.
work	He is going to work in his tractor.
your	Your baby is wearing a yellow suit.
about	It's about to be 12:30.

Read
Trace
Write
after
नंतर
again
पुन्हा
apple
सफरचंद
black
काळा
bread
ब्रेड
bring
आणा

Read and write the sentence!

after		The teacher calmed them after they fought.
again		He did it again!
apple		The apple is red and juicy.
black		The crow is black.
bread		My breakfast is bread and jam.
bring		He is bringing his project.

Read	Trace	Write
brown तपकिरी		
carry वाहून नेणे		
chair खुर्ची		
clean स्वच्छ		
could करू शकता		
don't करू नका		

Read and write the sentence!

brown		Her stuffed animal is a brown bear.
carry		He is carrying a big crayon.
chair		He is sitting on his chair.
clean		He needs to clean up.
could		The baby could do push-ups.
don't		Don't do that!

Read
Trace
Write
drink
पेय
eight
आठ
every
प्रत्येक
first
पहिला
floor
मजला
found
आढळले

Read and write the sentence!

drink	The baby likes to drink water.
eight	You get eight gifts for turning eight!
every	Every book is colorful.
first	We won first place.
floor	She is sitting on the floor.
found	It found a hat in the streets.

Read
Trace
Write
funny
मजेदार
going
जा
grass
गवत
green
हिरवा
horse
घोडा
house
घर

Read and write the sentence!

funny

The rabbit thinks the joke is funny.

going

The bear is going to eat all the honey.

grass

The goat eats grass on the hill.

green

The turtle that is walking is green.

horse

The horse is magical.

house

They lived in that house.

Read
Trace
Write
kitty
मांजर
laugh
हसणे
light
प्रकाश
money
पैसे
never
कधीही नाही
night
रात्री

Read and write the sentence!

kitty	The kitties are charming.
laugh	They are laughing while playing.
light	The boy will turn on the lights.
money	I have earned a lot of money.
never	The bear never ate ice cream before.
night	I will sleep on my blanket at night.

Read	Trace	Write

Read and write the sentence!

Read
Trace
Write
sheep
मेंढी
sleep
झोप
small
लहान
start
प्रारंभ करा
stick
लाठी
table
टेबल

Read and write the sentence!

sheep	The sheep have a bell around its neck.
sleep	I will go to sleep in my comfortable bed.
small	The small baby will crawl to its crib.
start	She will start sleeping soon.
stick	He has some sticks to play.
table	The table has a toy on it.

Read
Trace
Write
thank
धन्यवाद
their
त्यांचे
there
तेथे
these
या
thing
गोष्ट
think
विचार करा

Read and write the sentence!

thank	He made a Thank you card for you.
their	They will enjoy their picnic.
there	There is something in front of you.
these	These are my eating material.
thing	The thing is broken.
think	She thinks about what she is going to draw.

Read
Trace
Write
those
त्या
three
तीन
today
आज
under
अंतर्गत
watch
पहा
water
पाणी

Read and write the sentence!

those	Those are mine.
three	She will turn three today.
today	Today is a beautiful day.
under	The puppy sleeps under the blanket.
watch	They both watch the video.
water	He is drinking water after a long soccer game.

Read	Trace	Write

Read and write the sentence!

where	Where are we?
which	The clothes which are my sisters are colorful.
white	The sheep have white wool.
would	He would tell them a story.
write	I like to write lots of stories.
always	I am always happy that it is Christmas.

Read	Trace	Write
around सुमारे	around	
before आधी	before	
better चांगले	better	
farmer शेतकरी	farmer	
father वडील	father	
flower फूल	flower	

Read and write the sentence!

around		I will shuffle the shapes around.
before		Before I go to school, I kiss my mom.
better		I can make it better.
farmer		The farmer takes care of the animals.
father		My father is wearing a blue shirt.
flower		She will play with the flowers.

Read
Trace
Write
garden
बाग
ground
ग्राउंड
letter
अक्षरे
little
थोडे
mother
आई
myself
मी

Read and write the sentence!

garden	Her garden is vast and healthy.
ground	I am playing with my dog on the ground.
letter	These are the letters A, B, and C.
little	The world is small.
mother	My mother is very nice.
myself	I made these by myself.

Read	Trace	Write
please कृपया		
pretty सुंदर		
rabbit ससा		
school शाळा		
sister बहीण		
street रस्ता		

Read and write the sentence!

please	Please stop pulling my hair.
pretty	She made the cake very pretty.
rabbit	The rabbit is white and soft.
school	This is the school.
sister	My sister is wearing a pink dress.
street	They are walking across the street.

Read	Trace	Write
window विंडो		
yellow पिवळा		
because कारण		
brother भाऊ		
chicken कोंबडी		
goodbye निरोप		

Read and write the sentence!

window		The window is open.
yellow		The ducky is yellow.
because		She will sleep because it is night.
brother		His brother is playing with him.
chicken		The chicken has hatched out of the egg.
goodbye		The animal is saying goodbye.

Read	Trace	Write
morning सकाळी		
picture चित्र		
birthday वाढदिवस		
children मुले		
squirrel गिलहरी		
together एकत्र		

Read and write the sentence!

morning		He likes to ride his bike in the morning.
picture		He will take a picture.
birthday		Today is my birthday!
children		The children are doing something.
squirrel		The squirrel is cute.
together		They are sharing a bed together.

www.ingramcontent.com/pod-product-compliance
Lightning Source LLC
Chambersburg PA
CBHW080839160726
47999CB00009B/2950